For the *Love* of the Bulldogs

An A–to–Z Primer for Bulldogs Fans of All Ages

Written by Frederick C. Klein
Illustrated and designed by Mark Anderson

On January 30, 1892, the University of Georgia played its first football game, beating Mercer College 50–0. Since this auspicious beginning, Georgia football has captivated the hearts and minds of fans for nearly 120 years. *For the Love of the Bulldogs* captures this rich tradition with an unforgettable trip though the alphabet highlighting the greatest players, coaches, traditions, and landmarks in Georgia football history.

Herschel Walker, Vince Dooley, Fran Tarkenton, and Knowshon Moreno are just a few of the personalities that you will encounter on the pages that follow. And while you remember those shining stars, treat yourself to the full Georgia football experience. Walk under the Arch. Sing "Glory, Glory." Imagine the sun on your face during an autumn afternoon at Sanford Stadium.

No wonder it's so easy to fall in love with the Bulldogs.

"A" is for the Arch,

Which beckons every grad
To its place in old Athens;
Son, daughter, and granddad.

The Arch, the traditional entrance to the University of Georgia's campus, was installed in 1864. Lore has it that any freshman who passes under it will never graduate, but some do anyway. The university was incorporated in 1785 as the nation's first state-chartered institution of higher learning. It now has 15 colleges and schools and a total enrollment of about 33,000 students.

"B" is for Butts,

The "Little Round Man."

His Georgia elevens

All had a good plan.

Wally Butts came to the university in 1938 as an assistant football coach under Joel Hunt and remained as the head coach for 22 years (1939–1960). Under Butts' direction Bulldogs teams won 140 games and four Southeastern Conference championships and made six bowl-game appearances. His 1942 team won 11 of 12 games and was named national champion in several polls. His 1946 squad went 11–0 and gained similar acclaim.

"C" is for Champ,

Who was something to see;

He'd catch 'em on "O"

And pound 'em on "D."

Champ Bailey, from Folkston, Georgia, was a modern-day throwback to the one-platoon era, a two-way performer who excelled on both sides of the ball. In 1998 he played cornerback well enough to receive the Bronko Nagurski Award as the nation's best collegiate defensive player—while also catching passes and returning kicks for the offense. He went on to have a brilliant professional football career as a defensive back with the Washington Redskins and Denver Broncos.

"D" is for Dye,

He starred in the line,

Then defected to Auburn

Where he coached just fine.

Pat Dye was a two-time All-American guard for the Bulldogs (1967–1968) who helped the 1968 team win the SEC championship and earn an Orange Bowl victory over Missouri. He later went into coaching and eventually guided Georgia's archrival, Auburn, to four SEC titles and seven wins over the Dogs during his 1981–1992 tenure as head football coach.

"E" is for

Edwards,

Who came for the shoes,
But stayed on to give
Opponents the blues.

Dan Edwards grew up poor in Gatesville, Texas, around the time of World War II. Lee McKinney, a former Georgia football player stationed with the army at Fort Hood near the town, saw him play and recruited him for the Bulldogs. As an incentive, McKinney took the young man to the fort's store and bought him a new pair of shoes. Edwards went on to star at end in Athens for the unbeaten 1946 team and captained the 1947 unit that went to the Gator Bowl. He was an All-American that last season.

"F" is for

Frankie Sinkwich,

Who, way back when,

Brought victory to Athens

And a prize for his den.

Sinkwich came to Georgia from Youngstown, Ohio, to become a three-year star for the Bulldogs and the Heisman Trophy winner with the school's 1942 national champs. A tailback who was equally adept running and passing, he accumulated more than 4,500 yards of total offense over his career and accounted for 60 touchdowns—30 each way. His uniform No. 21 is one of four that the university has retired.

"G" is for

"Glory, Glory,"

The Bulldogs' fight song.

From the first time you hear it

You must sing along.

Sung to the tune of "The Battle Hymn of the Republic," "Glory, Glory" is one of the nation's best-known college fight songs and is certainly the easiest to learn. Its words are as follows: "Glory, glory to old Georgia/Glory, glory to old Georgia/Glory, glory to old Georgia/G-E-O-R-G-I-A."

"H" is for Hoage
Hearst.

And Garrison

In their turns they led

The Bulldogs to first.

Terry Hoage was a defensive back who played on teams that had a record of 43–4–1 and won two SEC titles in his four years at Georgia (1980–1983). He was a consensus All-American in 1982 and 1983, and an Academic All-American as well. Garrison Hearst was a running back who led the Dogs in rushing in each of his three seasons (1990–1992). In 1992 he won the Doak Walker Award as the nation's best college running back. His 3,232 yards gained on the ground is second on the school's all-time list.

"I" is a letter
You won't find in team.
Success on the gridiron means
Following one scheme.

"J" is for

Jake_

This Scott sure was slick.

When the other guys passed

He'd leap for a "pick."

Jake Scott played two seasons in Athens (1967 and 1968) and led the SEC in pass interceptions both years. Despite his brief stay, the defensive back's 16 total "picks" and 315 return yards are the most for any Georgia player. Vince Dooley once called him the best athlete he'd ever coached. Scott went on to have an excellent pro football career with the Miami Dolphins and Washington Redskins, appearing in six consecutive Super Bowls.

"K" is for Knowshon—

A yardage explosion!
Give him the ball and
His backfield's in motion.

Knowshon Moreno was Georgia's best running back since Herschel Walker. As a redshirt freshman in 2007 the New Jersey native gained 1,334 yards and was named SEC freshman of the year. He topped that in 2008 by running for 1,400 yards and earning All-SEC and All-America honors. His prowess as a pass receiver increased his value to his teams.

"L" is for

Larry Munson,

Whose voice on the air

Meant the Bulldogs were playing

Some football somewhere.

Munson was the Bulldogs' primary radio voice for more than 40 years beginning in 1966; his deep, throaty voice became synonymous with Georgia football. Munson was an unapologetic "homer" who lived and died with the team and was a noted fashioner of repeatable lines. "Who do we sue if we had a stroke?" he once asked his audience during an especially tense game.

"M" is for McWhorter,

A back for the ages.

He put Georgia football

On the nation's sports pages.

Bob McWhorter was a four-year starter at halfback for the Bulldogs (1910–1913) and a four-time All-Southern Conference selection. He was Georgia's first football All-American (in 1913) and the first student to captain both the football and baseball teams. He earned Phi Beta Kappa honors as an undergraduate, turned down a professional baseball contract to go to law school, and returned to the Georgia campus to teach law for 33 years. Four times he was elected mayor of Athens.

"N" is for Nash,

Of "Dream and Wonder" acclaim.

His team beat old Yale

In '27's big game.

Tom Nash was a star end on the "Dream and Wonder" team of 1927, the first Georgia eleven to defeat mighty Yale in the "Battle of the Bulldogs" series that began four years earlier. The '27 Dogs gained attention by starting their season with nine straight wins before losing to Georgia Tech, but received national-championship votes nonetheless. Nash played both professional football and baseball after graduation, then went home to Washington, Georgia, for a life as a businessman, teacher, coach, and court official.

"O" is for "Oh, my!"

The Dogs' fans' exclamation,

When Lindsay Scott won the race

That shocked the Gator Nation.

Perhaps the most famous play in Georgia football history came on November 8, 1980, in a crucial game between the Bulldogs and Florida at Jacksonville. Georgia came in with an 8–0 record compared to Florida's 6–1, but the Gators led 21–20 with less than two minutes left in the game and Georgia 92 yards from the end zone. Two plays resulted in the loss of a yard. Then quarterback Buck Belue found split-end Lindsay Scott with a pass near the Georgia 25-yard line and Scott outran the gasping Gators the rest of the way to score and secure a 26–21 victory. Georgia would win its next three games and claim the national crown.

"P" is for

Pollack—

On defense, a rock.

Foes found this big fellow

Just too tough to block.

David Pollack, from Snellville, Georgia, was the most decorated lineman in Bulldog football annals, a three-time All-American defensive end who gathered numerous conference and national prizes during his 2001–2004 career. Among those were the SEC Player of the Year Award in 2002 and the 2004 Vince Lombardi Award, given to the top collegiate lineman who best embodied the late coach's standards of discipline. Known for his quickness and pursuit, Pollack holds the school record for quarterback sacks with 36.

"Q" is for the

Quarterbacks—

Stafford, Tarkenton, and Greene.

They're about the best trio

The game's ever seen.

Georgia has a history of great quarterbacks but Matthew Stafford, Fran Tarkenton, and David Greene stand out even in that company. Stafford was a three-year starter (2006–2008) who was widely acclaimed as having the nation's best collegiate passing arm. His 25 touchdown passes in 2008 is a school record. Tarkenton led the Bulldogs to the 1959 SEC title, then turned the "scramble" into an art form during a brilliant NFL career. With Greene at the controls, Georgia won the 2002 SEC crown. He holds school records for career passing yards (11,538), pass completions (849), and touchdown passes (72).

"R" is for the

Rivalries,

That make football great,

Because everyone needs

Somebody to hate.

Georgia has been blessed with three traditional rivalry games, each of which is the equal of any in college football. The Bulldogs versus Auburn is one of the South's oldest football matchups, dating from 1892. Auburn held a 53–51–8 edge through 2007. Georgia-Florida, played on the "neutral" ground of Jacksonville, Florida, has been billed as "the world's largest outdoor cocktail party"; the Bulldogs have a 47–38–2 advantage in that one. The in-state rivalry with Atlanta-based Georgia Tech goes back to 1893, with Georgia leading 59–37–5. When asked, many Bulldogs fans are hard-pressed to say which of those three foes they dislike most. "All three," is the usual answer.

"S" is for

Sanford Stadium,

Where Dawgs fans hold sway.

A better sports venue

You won't find today.

Named for Dr. Steadman V. Sanford, the university's president at the time, Sanford Stadium opened on October 12, 1929, with an overflow crowd of about 30,000 people watching as the Bulldogs beat Yale. It since has been expanded to hold 92,746 people, making it one of the nation's largest venues. Their winning percentage of close to 75 percent attests to the home support the Bulldogs receive.

"T" is for Trippi,

A Coal Country lad.

For the team in the '40s

He gave all he had.

Charley Trippi came to Georgia from the coal-mining town of Pittston, Pennsylvania, after being recruited by ex-Bulldogs lineman Harold Ketron. The shifty halfback starred for the 1942 Georgia team that won 11 of 12 games including the Rose Bowl, went into the Air Force for two and a half years, then returned to Athens to play in 1945 and 1946. The Dogs went unbeaten that last year and Trippi won the Maxwell Award as the nation's best college player. A fine all-around athlete, he later played both professional football and baseball.

"U" is for

Uga,

Wrinkly, sturdy, and fun.

He makes Sanford Stadium

The world's largest dog run.

Uga, the bulldog, is one of America's best-known and most-loved college mascots, a symbol of Georgia's athletic tenacity since 1956. The current holder of the name is the seventh in a line of purebred white English bulldogs. He got the job in 2008, taking over after the passing of Uga VI, who had presided over more wins (87) than any of the mascots and at 65 pounds had been the biggest Uga of all.

"V" is for

Vince Dooley,

Who made the team go,

Then moved on upstairs

And ran the whole show.

Vince Dooley was Georgia's head football coach from 1964 through 1988, the longest stretch anyone has held the position. He also was the most successful, with a 201–77–10 record, a national championship (1980), six SEC titles, and 20 bowl-game appearances. He became Georgia's athletics director in 1979 and kept that post until 2004. The school's teams thrived under his leadership.

"W" is for

Walker,

A ball-carrier supreme.

For size, strength, and speed

He was every coach's dream.

Herschel Walker from Wrightsville, Georgia, was arguably the best college running back ever, a player who packed power and speed in equally high quantities. He burst onto the scene as a freshman in 1980 by gaining 1,610 yards rushing and leading the Bulldogs to the national title. His next two seasons were even more productive, and his career total of 5,259 rushing yards is a school record—even though he played only three years. He was a three-time All-American and won the Heisman Trophy in 1982. In 1999 CBS named him the best college offensive player of the 20th century. He was selected to the Walter Camp Foundation's All-Century first team.

"X" is a mark

Coaches make in a book.

Georgia has given plenty

Of those guys a look.

The Bulldogs have had many distinguished makers of "Xs" and "Os" besides Wally Butts and Vince Dooley. **Glen "Pop" Warner, the greatest coach of the game's early days, guided the team in 1895 and 1896 and posted an unbeaten (4–0) record the last year. George "Kid" Woodruff won two-thirds of his games and the 1927 Southern Conference title during his 1923–1927 tenure. Ray Goff (1989–1995) and Jim Donnan (1996–2000) each had solid winning marks. Current coach Mark Richt, a former offensive coordinator at Florida State, came aboard in 2001 and never has had a losing season at Georgia. His record at the school through 2008 was 82–22. His teams won SEC championships in 2002 and 2005, and his 2008 squad went 10–3 with a victory over Michigan State in the Capital One Bowl.**

"Y" is for the year
When we led the band;
The 1980 Bulldogs
were best in the land.

The 1980 team, led by Herschel Walker, quarterback Buck Belue, and cornerback Scott Woerner, was Georgia's best ever. It went through its regular season with 11 straight victories and beat Notre Dame in the Sugar Bowl to secure the consensus ranking as national No. 1.

"Z" is for

Zambiasi,

A linebacker with grit.

He'd track down a runner

And lay on a big hit.

Ben Zambiasi, from Macon, Georgia, was a three-year starter for the Bulldogs (1975–1977). Neither very tall (6-foot-1) nor very heavy (about 210 pounds) by football standards, he nonetheless graduated as the school's all-time tackles leader with 467 and gained All-SEC honors as a junior and senior. Vince Dooley said he never coached "a more intense and tenacious football player."

Purchase high-quality 18x24 archival prints
of your favorite Bulldogs at:

This book is available in quantity at special discounts for your group or organization. For further information, contact:

Triumph Books
542 South Dearborn Street
Suite 750
Chicago, Illinois 60605
312. 939. 3330
Fax 312. 663. 3557
www.triumphbooks.com

Printed in China
ISBN 978–1–60078–135–3